Praise f

C000064901

"Rain and the river
poems by Tyler Rober. .... ris writing is clean, clear,
and as accessible as Jane Kenyon's and Mary Oliver's, but
beneath the surface of these poems runs a vein of pure
linguistic gold. There are no slack moments in this book.
Each piece surprises and satisfies with brilliant images and
word choices. After a Night on the Sandbar, we hear "...the
hum of dark water, the sizzle of stars." Beautiful language.
So simple. So enjoyable. This writer knows the river, "...
bucks under the weight of its rider." that (the river) "At
night it shakes its long mane. Often, we are surprised with
such beauty. After dinner "...lights in the restaurant are
warm as midafternoon sun. You are back in the world, and
all the world is pleased" as will be the readers of this superb
and engrossing collection.

> -R. Nikolas Macioci, author of *Why Dance?* and
> *Dark Guitar*

"In his new collection *When to Ask for Rain* Tyler Robert
Sheldon writes about the common things in his life but with
a poet's eye. He weaves this subtle yet powerful collection
together by taking us on a journey into his classroom,
through Louisiana and by providing vivid snapshots of
floating and camping on the river. This poetry is not in
your face but it is almost something that we should already
know and relayed to the reader in a gentle voice and tone.
When to ask for Rain is a refreshing new collection of poetry
that when you read it for the second and third time you will
discover what you may have forgotten. It is the journey and
what you do with it."

> -Scot Young, author of *All Around Cowboy*

More praise for Tyler Robert Sheldon:

"These sharp-focused vignettes and portraits of people and places slow us into moments that upend, delight, and sometimes alarm us, as Sheldon proposes that 'learning is often like instant photography where we all must be shaken awake.' The careful craft of these poems carries the reader into rain-drenched Louisiana streets 'full of good luck and trouble,' and upstream to muddy midwestern rivers alive with hidden fossils and finds. This brilliant, alluvial collection explores the ways we make communion, the ways we trace ourselves back towards a source, the way our waters combine, become one story brimming with legends, ancient arrowheads, and the one that got away."

-Amy Sage Webb-Baza, author of *Save Your Own Life: Kansas Stories*

"In this wonderfully watery poetry collection, Tyler Robert Sheldon looks and listens with sincerity. Whether as a newcomer to the Deep South, a teacher, or a seeker of artifacts, Sheldon interrogates the liminal spaces where meaning can be found, and his readers are the wiser for the discoveries shared in these finely wrought poems."

-Amy Fleury, author of *Sympathetic Magic*

WHEN TO ASK FOR RAIN

Poems by Tyler Robert Sheldon

Spartan
Press

Spartan Press

Kansas City, Missouri

spartanpress.com

Copyright © Tyler Robert Sheldon, 2021

First Edition: 1 3 5 7 9 10 8 6 4 2

ISBN: 978-1-952411-62-5

LCCN: 2021936653

Cover image: Jim McGowin

Author photo: Alex Arceneaux

ACKNOWLEDGEMENTS

My deep gratitude to Thomas Fox Averill, Sammie Bellavia, James Benger, Brian Daldorph, Amy Fleury, Jessica Frank, J. Bruce Fuller, Martha Garner, Albert Goldbarth, Kal Heck, Sadie Hutchison, John Jenkinson, Allison Joseph, Kelli Scott Kelley, Jami Kleinpeter, Ted Kooser, Marcia Lawrence, Keagan LeJeune, Ashlee Lhamon, Denise Low, R. Nikolas Macioci, Clare L. Martin, Deb and Terry Maxwell, Patrice Melnick, Caryn Mirriam-Goldberg, Lisa Moritz, Stephen and Taryn Möller Nicoll, Dan Pohl, Jeanette Powers, Kevin Rabas, Michelle Romero, Beth Scroggins, Bessie Senette, Kim Stafford, Jon Tribble, Amy Sage Webb-Baza, Sue Weinstein, Walter Welch, Sharon Weltman, Sarah Ann Winn, Scot Young and Trudy Zimmerman.

With love to all my family, my greatest teachers. And to Harley Elliott, Steven Hind, and Scott Brown, river-walkers.

Thanks to my Louisiana neighbors and friends, who appear (somewhat fictionalized) in several of these poems. It'd be a far less interesting neighborhood without you. And to my students: remember your academic voice and keep up your good work. I'm proud of what you do.

Finally, I'm grateful to the editors of the following publications, in which some of these poems, sometimes in other versions, first appeared: *365 Poems in 365 Days Anthology, I-70 Review, The Midwest Quarterly, Mocking Heart Review, Now Then Manchester, The Pangolin Review, Quiddity International Literary Journal, Louisiana Literature, Red Eft Review, San Pedro River Review, Thorny Locust, Tittynope Zine,* and *Yes, Poetry.*

"Rice Palace," "Conversations in Hurricane Season," and "At the Court of Two Sisters" first appeared in *Driving Together* (Meadowlark Books, 2018).

TABLE OF CONTENTS:

I. Pelican State Memos

II. River

III. Ghost Story

For Alex, with my heart

PELICAN STATE MEMOS

WHEN TO ASK FOR RAIN

Our neighborhood once flooded so severely
the huge dumpster at the apartment's edge,
green and rusted through with age,
lifted itself on the leaf-bearing gray water
and wobbled across the broken concrete lot.

No matter how we pushed, it turned our way,
floating by the front door or our car,
threatening destruction. We could hear
the neighborhood cats mewling,
caught out in the sudden rain.

That night the water crept away.
The great green dumpster stuck like a warning
to the cracked concrete outside, witnessing
and unafraid. Inch by inch we slowly crunched
that bin across the lot, grunting at the effort.

The cats began again to circle round the bin,
mewling and content, surveying. They too
had seen just how swiftly it had moved.
We laughed and shook our heads.
We asked for just a little rain.

LEARNING THE NEIGHBORHOOD

Old South Baton Rouge

I.
Here the rent is cheap
and there are iron bars on the windows.
This means at some point the landlord
learned from experience. You know
eventually to not look up
for the echo of gunshots downstreet.
When a woman screams
you turn the key quietly
in the iron gate before your door
and sip your coffee quieter than before.

II.
All the city's rain eventually finds a way here.
Jeff, graduate student, lost his old car
in last year's flood. He lives upstairs.
All my stuff was fine, he says,
but that car is a replacement. I don't tell him
about my barely-there insurance, or
say how weather doesn't wait for paychecks.
But he smiles as if he knows my mind.

III.
Neighborly advice: this block
is the one pocket of safety in the city.
If you go past Roosevelt, walk there only
in the daytime. At night no one will come
to help you. But don't think too hard
about it. Everything will be just fine.

MEETING GIGI

We see her when the big tree breaks
its arms into the next-door yard:
our first neighbor, her bright eyes
lightning-quick to pick up
the whole neighborhood.

Two huge limbs sit on the power line
above us. Alex gets a big stick,
passes to me, says get them off that wire,
and behind me the neighbor plays
with her fresh-cut hair: *I'm goin'*
for kind of red, see? Her short curls
are fire-orange, tight to scalp.
She dresses hair, she says,
in her very own salon.

She tells us call her *Gigi,*
the whole block does: the kids
who crowd her yard to hear the news,
the customers who come to see her.

She says, y'all need anything, let me know.
Just don't trust those meth heads
behind your place.   In the apartment
behind ours, she tells us loudly,
there's a woman who asked her
for groceries right after moving in.

I move the heavy stick again.
The branches swing a little on the line.
She can go to goddamn Walmart, Gigi says.

LAKE CHARLES

In the city where I teach each morning,
two hours west, you can buy a daiquiri
from a drive-thru on the corner.
Scotch tape on top makes it
a perfectly legal closed container.
The cashier might palm you a straw.

The Texans who drive here for work
are brash outside their home fences. They
swing into the bike lanes (really sidewalks),
still safer most times than the street.

Some days you can watch police cars
on their way to Friendly Donuts
from the top floor of the building
where I show others how to tango
with semicolons and virgules.

Law firms and churches dot the streets
that circle town, signs of warning
for those who do wrong here, and
those at the receiving end. Learning
is often like instant photography
where we all must be shaken awake.

GWEN

On our first full day in Baton Rouge
we see Gwen walk her husband's wheelchair
out front. Busted glass sits there tarped,
tied to the canvas seat. Gwen lives
around back, and needs help lifting
this tarp to the trash. *I broke a table,*
she says. *One of its legs busted. Then the top.*
I tell her it's lucky some glass shatters.
Lucky she's not cut. We lift and tip and shake.

Once done she pushes the wheelchair back,
huge tires stumping over busted bricks.
Next day she's at our door to sell
high heels, two pointed shoes on sticks.
They're fifty-dollar shoes, she says.
Maybe they'll fit your wife. They sit there,
small and red in the wheelchair as I say no.

Next door, soon, there's knocking.
Gwen wheels those high heels all around.

LESSONS

Monday
A student pulls me aside to talk.
He's joining the Army Reserve,
won't be submitting his final project.
He proceeds to miss every class
without another word.

Tuesday
I grade. One student, to meet the word count,
has a page of extra words in white font:
mock-invisible, all of them nonsense.
The rest: too short to count
for much. He writes: *I sure hope
this doesn't affect my grade!*

Wednesday
I show the class online research.
We talk about the death penalty.
The lights are off all class.
One student says, *wow,
this sure is dark*. I wonder
just what he means.

Thursday
For an attendance question,
I ask what the class will do
after college. They think
hard. Only a few begin

to write. One student says,
Why do you always ask
such hard questions?

Friday
They for once refuse my offer
to start the weekend
a few minutes early. We
have lots to talk about,
they say. Join us.
Let's talk.

GUNSHOTS

I meet another neighbor
by the mailboxes out front,
with his dreadlocks and gold grin:
another wheelchaired man,
with wire-strong arms.
We drink coffee together. He says
he used to run the streets, used to
do bad things, bad things.

He says he used to be
vicious Tyrone.

He asks me if I've even
been shot. *I've been shot
three times,* he says, *and
the first one was right here.*

Tyrone points back behind himself,
right beside the spine. *I couldn't
feel my legs for days,* he says.
Then came pain.

He gestures to where those legs
had been. Waist up only, there's
Tyrone.   *It was bone
disease that took these,*

he says, *the sort of thing*
nobody ever gets but me.
Wasn't those gunshots. Those
bullets couldn't touch me
that deep, from inside.

Worst, I gave away my shoes,
he says. *Brand new sneaks,*
with that cool pump, and they
would've stayed new in this chair.
Those bullets put me there,
he says. But part of me stayed out.

MY STUDENTS' WHEELBARROWS

after B.C. and W.C.W.

One by one they trickle to their seats.
They expect a day of scribbling
in their notebooks what they're only
pretending to think, but I tell them,
it is finally the time to have our talk
about poetry.

I tell them, look here at how Williams breaks
his lines, so unlike Shakespeare, and one,
her hand above the sea of heads, tells us
they're wheelbarrows. You can lift
these lines and even pivot, if you wish.
She drops her hand and just like that
the silence breaks.

Another stands to speak: white, he says,
means purity. For the rest, so much depends
upon these words. All they want to do
is tie chickens to that color
so they won't escape.

When they finally trickle out, talk shifts
back to other things. A few leave
with pens in hand. I turn off the lights.
Beyond our classroom, the trees
are glazed with rain.

THE ATTORNEY

next door to our apartment is wild
about dogs. Her Rottweiler leaps
against the fence, and growls
when I take out the trash. *This is Cat,*
she says, *and he won't hurt you.*
She scratches this fearsome pup
behind the ears. He calms.
For now, for him, I'm just okay.

She works animal cruelty cases, and sees
dogs at the ends of roads, the ends
of driveways, of their canine minds.
She likes them better than people,
who she says know exactly how
to be cruel to fill their time. *Dogs don't
hurt you unless made to,* she says.
But when she goes in Cat stays.
He watches me. I back away,
just another newbie on his turf.

CLASS AFTER MARDI GRAS

The students who show bring evidence:
Jeans torn from a morning hunt, sand that cakes
the carpet gray around their shoes,
knuckles scraped by the oarlocks
of a father's fishing boat. They bring half
their drafts, chains of green and purple beads,
photos they grin over furtively,
tilted away from me on their phones.

We joke about the drinking age. We circle up
the desks. One student spent the entire week
chasing chickens with family in a town not far
from here. An old tradition. Their hands shake
around pens and pencils pulled from backpacks.
We are so very tired, they say. Then they begin
to write. They journal about their favorite floats,

the best trinkets thrown to the late-night street.
Some fought off drunken partygoers for doubloons.
A few have these on their desks, bright plastic coins
reflecting fluorescent classroom light. When we
let out early, they leave one on my desk. *It's good
to spread the luck around,* one students says.
We leave. Fortune follows after down the hall.

TRUNK

Gigi, our first neighbor, wants to go dumpster diving.
It's almost dark out, and by this point she's taken us
through the mountains and valleys of her house: antique
headboards, an old neon "Open" sign—this she's put
in her front window, not the advice I'd give to *my* neighbors
—and a giant plasma TV that takes so long to warm up
you could make a sandwich, so she says. These, and even
other dubious treasures. All of it, yes *all* of it, found out
by the street. *People give away their lives,* she says. *I help them.*

She takes us down the block and points out two gigantic
industrial dumpsters. We hoist her in to one and then
follow her over the side. Gigi holds her nose, sifts clothes,
wrappers, furniture; she finds a hulking metal clothes rack,
grabs it. My wife spies a giant box, a pressboard trunk.
I see its load of musty clothes, castoffs from folks moved on
and grown past them. These we dig out of our way,
and we haul the old trunk out, down to the sidewalk.
We carry it back down the block: massive, swinging, full
of dust, furniture readymade, exactly what we need.

TO MY COMPOSITION STUDENTS

Please understand that when
you don't turn in an essay, the first
thing I think of is your well-being.
If you've gotten sick I understand.
We all do. But if you're so out of it
that an email taxes you, I'll
certainly lose a little sleep.

Please understand, I don't like you less
for showing up late, while I'm talking.
Respect is another matter. Also, no.
I can't give you an extension just
because you helped a friend move.
I know it's hard, but this class
is an airplane: when the masks drop

save yourself first. Please understand
that extra credit means just that.
While a child you learned the rules
of dessert. You will learn that this
is much the same. you don't get
anything extra until you finish
all of your regular credit.

When you raise a hand to speak,
understand that it makes me sit
up straighter. Know that you all
are teachers, whether you like it

or not. And try to understand
that turbulence is perfectly normal
and airplanes nearly always level out.

CONVERSATIONS IN HURRICANE SEASON

Even though it's sometimes safer to go north
as far as possible, mandatory evacuation
doesn't mean you *have* to leave. Really,
if your home is elevated it might be enough
to sit there for a while in the dark

when the power goes out—and it *will*
go out—and the neighbor's truck floats
past your living room. When it gets hot
just remember that sweating is good for you
and still better than an August power bill.

I am likely a terrible person to hope
that the Carolinas or maybe Florida
will get the worst of it. That way
our streets will be completely dry
and nothing but the usual.

Afterward we can all walk outside
and say that things are normal, that
next time will certainly happen
somewhere else, where
next times always do.

MULTIPLE CHOICE

I.

He went to buy a new car.
It was raining. He canceled
his other appointments
because of the rain and stayed in
to watch movies he hated.

II.

He bought a new car. It rained
as he went off to rent a movie
he knew that he would hate. He'd never
seen the movie but that's what
everyone promised would happen.

III.

He bought a movie and quickly
discovered he hated it. Everyone
in the movie had a new car.
He liked the cars but hated the movie.

IV.

He starred in a movie
and his character got a new car.
He learned that he hated the movie
because he had to wreck the car.
He had loved that car. He walked
away from the car in the rain.

HIGHWAY LANGUAGE

after William Stafford

Atchafalaya Swamp Freeway

Slowing down like this means
"Pass me now."

Keeping the posted speed means
"I have nowhere to be and am from nowhere."

Signaling to pass another means
"You won't recognize me."

Flashing brake lights mean
"Trouble ahead."

Blurring road lines mean
"Trouble close behind."

The sun reflecting rain like this means
"You are headed the right way."

RICE PALACE

Crowley, Louisiana

Businessmen
dark-suit late-night-shades men
crowd around the coffee counter
with round copper in their loafers
setting suns in brown leather

AT THE COURT OF TWO SISTERS

Downtown New Orleans

I haven't seen these streets in over a decade,
the bluesy vibrating pavement capped by
some of the country's oldest buildings. Our friend,
who has lived here for years, says it hasn't rained
in weeks, so we'll want to avoid the puddles.
Further in, there are more people dressed in silver paint.
Gas lamps burn and sputter against the dark.

A bar band grinds out Hoochie Coochie Man.
The guitar player sings deep in his gravelly voice.
He watches me watch him play, and nods through smoke.
On Rue Bourbon we stare at the sign that has seen
decades of drunken brawls and folklore
fade its finish, midnight black to tomcat gray.

At the Court we walk under a wisteria canopy
strung with lights, a single draping tree, and Taryn says
good wishes here protect you from what this town can do.
We throw three old pennies in the well. Then we weave
back to the street, full of good luck and trouble,
and the old town tightens back around us.

WEATHER SIGNS: A NEIGHBOR'S STORY

On the man's bike ride home it started to rain.
Big fat drops fell onto his glasses
and soaked into the seat of his pants.
This is surely a metaphor, thought the man.
Maybe I shouldn't have told such
nasty political jokes at the office today.
Lightning struck a taco truck in the distance.
The man pedaled harder.

At the stop light near his home
a spit cup chucked from a big truck
grazed his shoe. That's no doubt for
eating Fred's sandwich for lunch,
the man thought. He resolved
to buy Fred's lunch the next day.
The sun peeked out from behind some clouds.

When the man arrived home he brought
his dog inside and toweled it off
out of the rain. He told his wife he loved her.
A rainbow coughed its way to the sky.

The sun waited
behind quilted clouds
for the man's next move.

WRITING PROMPT

To see how surrealists
ease the pressure we all gather
by virtue of our living, take
your watch from the nightstand.
Carry it into that wide ship's hold
of thundered southern sky. Now hold it
aloft, a lightening lightning rod,
with your open and welcoming hands:
your own turning, circular
hot spot, your transient metal heart.

ODE TO THE FUGITIVE CRAWFISH

Little-claw, I know your legs
have climbed towers taller
than your fathers dared to dream.
You pulled them, countless,
upward in your armored hands.
Rainstorms cannot fathom
the earthen castles they must break
to break you, master architect.

You have escaped kitchens
told of only in hushed whispers
among the bravest of your kind.
You have foiled pets and brooms
and fled back to the wild in a cloak
of dust bunnies from where you fell
behind the deadly stove.

And little-claw, you
are the one nobody suspects.
Only you have hidden
so long from the seasoned pot.
No one has degloved you
from the asterisk of your tail.
We've said to all the others,
We've found you, boys.
your mounding days are over.

But never you. Keep running.
Build your towers higher
than the moon. We know you can.
We know. We know.

SOWELA RAINSTORM

Outside my classroom windows
it is raining straight down:

streaking liquid TV static.
It clatters on the roof tiles above,

nearly invisible in the weltering sky,
crackling through trees, against wind-

shields, and I wish
for just one umbrella full of holes.

I would run and jump and never
stop 'til my eyes and ears were full.

RIVER

RIVER'S PARABLE OF SELF

I.

The fisher who reels up a catch
in early morning's net winds different parts
of self into himself. The fish
has known this moment its whole life,
and is not afraid because nets are not afraid.
The river eddies around them all
and catches them, and is also caught.

II.

Rivers move mostly one way at once
to meet other parts of themselves
they already know.

III.

Whirlpools are rivers
remembering themselves.

FIRST HUNT

for my father

At the new site in Rice County
I am looking for artifacts
for the very first time. Dad and I
schlep our sharpened sticks, water bottles
across the long and wintering grass
to the sandbar. We stop every few minutes
to pluck bulbous sandburs from our socks.

Two hours in I find a cat skull
submerged in a puddle, sun-bleached,
grinning with scraps of small wickedness
from the gravel. I dust it carefully
and begin the climb to where Dad
bends down, something round
in his hand. He straightens, holds up

a dark stray thought of flint,
a bird point, one ear snapped
by flight or those long centuries in clay.
The tip is gone—a tiny flat plane,
paleolithic plateau, cross-section
all that remains. He grins. Each of us rich,
we walk slowly back through the stickers.

MOM, WHO KNOWS

how to navigate the river,
coaxes her yellow kayak
around the tree-fall
like she knew
long ago of its place
in how everything turns.

Her boat overturns
only once, and bobs in the river,
She rights it soon after treading in place,
and then casts a line from her kayak
that makes barely a new
ripple, barely a wobble: it falls

quick to the water, ready to haul
up our lunch. We take turns
casting lines into the new,
strong current. The river
brings itself level with the kayak,
deeper and fast. We quicken our pace.

At length we come to a dry place,
a gravel bar. We step overboard, feel
wet sand underfoot. Pull the kayak
aground, taking turns, onto this island
quite a way down the river.
We are tired like we never knew.

Later, near the shore: who knew
that there would be a place
on this churning river
where it is already fall?
We row swiftly past trees turned
the shade of Mom's kayak,

sun-yellow. She rows her kayak
aground and points to a new
visitor, who calls to us in turn:
a sparrow, perched high in a cedar.
Soon it hops into the air and falls
outward, gliding over the river.

Together we all turn the kayak
upward out of the river, newly
at home and at peace with it all.

WHAT THE RIVER NEEDS

Attention. Never bring
half your game
to the sandbar.
You will only miss
every moment,
which will be caught
by those around you
who are prepared.

Time. When you find
water moving oddly
beside you, look harder
as long as you must
for what it might mean.
The sun will still move,
but when night finds you
you will hear clearer
than the water ahead.

Patience. The best
bones, flint points,
pot shards come
to those who wait,
placing feet
rippleless
straight down,
never forward,
never through.

Sharp ears. All
who wish only
to hear an egret
will surely
hear everything
but an egret. Wait.
See *Patience*, above.
They will come
but you must listen.

Instinct. This
you must hone.
All leaves look
like worked arrows
under the current.
Pluck as many
as you must
from the water
until you find
blessed flint
in your fingers.
Memorize.
Give thanks.
Repeat.

SMALL FINDS

I.

We go down over the hip of the land
to the river, catching stickers in our jeans,
small stitches of pain in the fabric of our selves.

II.

Bottle-hunting, my spouse spies
a mud-dark ink well, deep in sand
by the bridge. At our coaxing
it releases, and we look for cracks,
maps of its time and its making.

III.

Tiny fish jump,
shocked away from each other,
Small static sparks.

STEVEN OF THE RIVER

I.

Flint-hunting, Dad and I hike downstream,
boots pushed along by shunting water,
eyes downcast toward flint we think we see,
often only leaves under the river's eddies.
Soon Steven, family friend in a Western shirt,

disappears past the curve ahead. We find him
reclined on the sandbar, feet propped
on a driftwood slab, black cowboy hat
slanted over his eyes. From paces away
I can begin to hear him snore.

II.

We almost run into him, stock still
in the water. He points slowly

toward a group of egrets on the bank,
blending best he can with the river

so they won't scatter, ruin
their perfect alignment.

Having no camera, we capture
all we can and then step away.

III.

Anything he finds he holds
silently, turning an open hand
to whoever's closest, letting
the point or scraper or chert flake
do the work; or else says only
look at that, soft like water,
then slips the piece into a pocket
and moves on.

RACCOON

Fish bandit waits,
eyes alert in dark bands,
for ripples within reach.
Flexes small hands.

RIVER

It bucks under the weight of its riders.
Some overbalance and scream
with joy at the suddenness of it,

relief falling like water
down their transcendent faces
as they learn to let go

and tumble down into the current,
bobbing up full of knowing.
All astride it are carried to safety.

Old lives are unearthed,
reborn under its racing.
At night it shakes its long mane.

HIGH STAKES

Under the river bridge I pick up a rock,
ask my father, who is upstream
just slightly, how much it's worth
to drill the heavy green pop bottle
hunched in the concrete-thrown shade.
He looks at the bottle, then back up
at me. He says: lunch, but one shot.
After that, we'll just have to see.

I'm a good twenty feet away
from this old glass bottle, buried
deep in its comfortable dirt,
dusty, dull. I cock back my arm,
take a step, heave with the rock.
It just nicks the top, taking off
part of the lip. Dad finds an old brick,
chucks it from the other side of the bridge,
and the green glass explodes,
bits flying into the dirt all around.

Later we grab lunch together,
shaking sand from the cuffs of our jeans
onto checkered taco joint tiles
for others to clean in our wake.

WHOSE TRACKS LEAD TO THE RIVER

The first inverse heart
pressed into earth
brings a question: *where*
will you go?
Past the edge of what I know,
speaks the second track
to the whispering grass, sunken
slightly further into dirt,
which shifts quietly
to sand.
Follow us, offer the next
two cloven hearts, whose edges
meet the sinking coast, the river's
eager hands. *We're here, we*
already know.
Goodbye, whispers
the deepest hoofprint
of the deer who lead us
to the river, calm
and slow.

SENTINEL BLACKBIRD

fans his red-tipped wings,
calls down from a cedar branch
the river's duties.

One could wait all day
for the sudden dark descent:
how feathers unfold,
the spokes of a small world
diving down through the bright trees.

When the river knows
its duty to keep the peace,
like a bird, it flows.

What the blackbird sees:
undulations in the air,
tremors that say *fly*,
that warn, *above you, look out.*
He tells everyone that's there.

Danger: close at hand
Until blackbird finds it out,
roots it from the land.

MUSIC

Because water captures sound
we think nothing of it
when small waves lap
our boat's edge in the night
like the heavy breath
of a maraca.

Because water keeps sound
to itself, we wait for rain
to plink out its short notes,
each higher than the last
upon the surface, and then
to send them strumming
over the rippled river
until they are so many
we cannot hear them.

Because water makes sound
secret, we listen close
and walk by the river.
We strain our ears
for small hints of the band,
for strings and woodwinds
stretching out like fingers
in a concert of dark sand.

KAYAK

I am here to save you. Believe it.
Nobody else knows how to keep you
upright in the water quite like me,

palindrome to outsmart all
that would unseat you, which as
you know is absolutely everything.

I know the heart-biting fury
of the treefall, can help you find
your way to back to empty water.

I am most capable. I require
only yourself and your courage,
nothing else, no one at all.

I am shaped like a knife blade
to cut through anything
that stands in your way.

TOO LATE TO SAVE

A water bottle floats
toward us on the river,
slips past the bow
of our boat. We paddle
back and find splashing,

the prow of the spare boat
sinking, full of our gear,
Dan treading water, hanging
one-handed to his own canoe.

As we right his listing boat,
gather coolers and tackle,
Dan cries out too late
as a whiskey fifth slips
beneath the surface.

WORDS AT EVENING

Owl hides in shore trees
coaxing us toward the dock
a mile or further
down our eddying river
part of the hastening night

NIGHT ON THE SANDBAR

We row all day, then beach the canoes
on a gravel bar far down the river.
Dan's been hard-rowing for hours
through treefalls and tall weeds,
lashed to the gear boat with sleep bags,
our grub, and the camp stove:
gear saved from sinking
by Dan's midday scramble,
the big boat unbalanced, turned over,
slowly righted. Now he falls half asleep,
almost in the fire we lead him to,
light coaxed to life on the edge of the bar.

James, his hands over the flames,
talks of how he'll wake us to bacon,
sizzled and crisp, how morning
will be here too soon.

Later James and I each
take one of Dan's shoulders,
rock him away from the fire
and onto his feet: Dan,
who saved all but his stamina
from a capsized canoe, collapses
to his sleeping bag, out.

Later, in gray predawn static:
a rumble of snoring, the hum
of dark water, the sizzle
of tentative stars.

ENCHILADAS AFTER STRIKING THE CAMP

You hoist open the door to a restaurant,
the three of you fresh from two days on the river,
burned red as bobbers from the reflected sun.
Dirt coats everything, socks to eyebrows.

The canoe will need to be scrubbed.
You will all need to be scrubbed. You
will wait too long and resign yourself
to scraping river mud from your shoes

slowly but it will be a meditation,
like the *hush, hush, hush* of paddles
through the river, which even now
continues its long walk.

You don't look up when the server leads
you to a table where you order enchiladas
and go off to wash your hands. This
takes too long so that the chips are cold

when you return. You don't speak
when the food comes, just fork bite
after bite like you've never eaten
in your life, like you just discovered the need.

Chairs scrape the floor a table away.
An old man laughs at some joke
like the bright wind-whistle of trees.
Your friends pass the chip basket,

and the lights in the restaurant
are warm as midafternoon sun.
You are back in the world,
and all of the world is pleased.

GHOST STORY

WHEN TO ASK FOR RAIN

When your lines are prepared
and braced deep in the promising dirt,
tilting from pole to bobber afloat on the surface,
red marker that moves and moves in the wind.

When the tent is up and your lantern waits
like an archer, eager for its chance
to pierce the lightening dove-gray sky.

When the earth around you, mouthless,
lets you know what it needs, dust rising
in eddies around the toes of your boots.

When you're back in the truck and out—
fully out—of the water, and the clouds
are finally ready at the edge of the sky,
waiting only to be let in.

PARTY OF HARLEQUINS

for Harley Elliott

I.

Harley, river-walker, tells me
in a letter he has cancer.
Not the tear-out-your-bones kind,
so he says, but the kind
that makes you think harder
than you ever have before.
He tells me he's begun to paint.

II.

The letter has Joker cards
printed on the back, collected
from years of decks. He makes
these pages himself, wry poet,
on a copy machine:
always six or eight cards,
a party of harlequins,
each keeping the others in check.

III.

A tuxedoed grinning man.
A sword juggler.
An empty, smoky bar.

Pain today
on every face.

DOG SKULL

Only this can be true:
any harsh hand trowel
must show proper respect
when it scoops its way down
into the hidden tomb.

When you excavate bones
it is better to go gently,
coaxing the yellowed past
from the dirt, where
it waits for its finding.

More sensible still,
first crack open the ground
around this, the end result
of some ancient dog's fight,
the winner long forgotten.

What of the owner,
whose small head slumbered,
relieved from its fighting
and covered through decades
with dark and muffling earth?

Only this: it will crouch
on your shoulder, waiting
for you. Has it come
to show you exactly how
you can help it?

OYSTER

We find you armored in the shallows,
clenched tightly under dark sand like a secret.
Here, the palisades of tight white barnacles
cling to you like pikemen, so little space
between each little soul you couldn't thread

a hair. And here, the layers of tiny plants
that waved as flags atop your shell,
gone still in the sudden, opened air
as when the wind removes itself.

We turn you over. On your back,
the channels of some robber
who would give their soul
to breach your walls but was not
strong enough to overtake you.

Inside, though it pains you more
than life itself, the beginnings
of a treasure you have learned
to coexist with—how strong you are!

All around you lies what's left
of others, their castles sieged
and plundered, broken often
by one small hole, one armor chink.
But here you are, small warrior,

your place is in the churn of things,
the waves of salt and night that sway
your little fortress like a prayer.
 It glimmers when we place you there.

MOUSE

Button of peripheral sound.
Student of outside corners.
Taster of wind and rain.
Guardian of the night.
Knower of danger.
Grass monger.
Hole-finder.
Borrower.
Alarm.
Run.

SLEIGHT OF HAND

My first wedding ring
spills from my finger
and into the drink
as soon as we flip the canoe.

I don't find this out
until we're back
in the sodden seats,
my hand empty of silver,

dark water laughing away
at the ribs of the boat.
Later I replace it,
just a few months old,

with a nicer band,
one I'll leave at home
when out on the river,
smoothest pickpocket of all.

GHOST STORY

I.

In the vault of the water
bones have patience
we can only imagine. The tops
of ossified bison teeth are zigs of bone
you will only see if you are lucky.
They hide. You must understand this
to learn the art of their finding.

These teeth, big as palms,
know the texture of small lives
no longer here.
One or two will crop us
on the river, small miracles
of time, and will wait
until you pass them,
looking down at just
the right moment,
pockets empty, eyes
downward in hope.

II.

Bones are mazes
of hollows, small clearings
where old movements
lie dormant. Can you
find the way?

ASSUMING DREAMS RESTORE OUR INNOCENCE

Our dog, from the water, jumps onto the sandbar.
He knows what to dig for, but yelps in surprise
when he finds it: a dark, ancient tire, rotted by time.
He drags it out for us, and down to the river.

He knows what to dig for, but yelps in surprise
when we don't attempt to share in his treasure
that he drags out for us and down to the river.
To him this is everything. If only we knew.

When we don't attempt to share in his treasure
he folds in his tail and sniffs at the driftwood:
to him, this is everything—if only we knew!
Half the wood in his teeth, he wades in the water.

He folds in his tail and sniffs at the driftwood.
We at last know to watch him, to smile and laugh:
half the wood in his teeth, he wades back to the water,
this good dog we've dreamed up in the dark.

We at last know to watch him, to smile and laugh
when he finds it: a dark, ancient tire, rotted by time.
This good dog we've dreamed up in the dark,
our dog, in the river, just his tracks on the sandbar.

REMEDIES

I.

If careful you can find bottles,
and old ones, on the banks
of the river. Ink wells and
green 7-Up glass that belongs
in some kind of museum.
Sand shelves bottles
of long-guzzled cola
and liquids more sinister still.

II.

Infant's Relief: chloroform,
cannabis indica, morphine
ethyl hydrochloride,
antimony, potassium tartrate.
White pine and tar.
All that's needed
for lingering cough.
Take one teaspoon
every three hours.

III.

Be so very glad
this cough syrup
is gone.

OLD FIELDS

for Harley Elliott

In a new letter, Harley
tells me he's still clean.
It's been a few years by now,
and in another he'll be free
of cancer, muscle-wasting,
endless drugs. He still paints
yards of canvas every day.

Harley's walked so many fields
he's got them alphabetized,
in different ink for good ones
and ones long since stripped
of arrow points and scrapers,
the fossil record of peoples past.
He calls one field the Rocking Deer,
says some new guy owns it
who won't return his calls,
but he remembers the treasure there,
buried under time and loam.

I tell him I remember
walking the river with him
and my father, inching upstream,
tired, and Harley chugging along
dogged in that field of water,
not to be curtailed.
We asked him how he felt:

Like a seventy-year-old man
up to his ass in goddamn water!
This is the best he'd been in years.

Today everything is different, Harley says.
The old fields are all new property,
cut off. But just one year
to go now. Won't be long.
When I'm free again, who knows.
We'll just have to wait and see.

ELEGY FOR ABANDONED RIVER POTTERY

Old ceramic, am I the only one
who knows you? Sun-dulled shards
of porcelain, this one flaunting
paisley, that one an edge that once
could slice a finger's pad and say,
I warned you not to. And this one,
you old tan finger-loop, so perfect
once for tipping back a jug at evening,
I mourn your amputated vessel.

These small slivers, black as bear's eyes,
silent little treasures, how many missed
your flash, your evening-wink,
when eager only for their trucks
waiting patient on the bank?
You owe not one of them a thing.

There is a reason why we're here:
to cradle you in an old shirt's pocket
or worn hat's band, to trek back with you
up the chilling autumn current
oh so slowly, eyes flicking
through the shunting water
for your lonely kin.

FOUR-WHEELER

I eat everything
before you have half a chance
to find it yourself.

Listen: my rumble
means birdsong is history,
peace is a mirage.

My tracks shatter hope
for civilizations past
to be found in sand.

The deep awe of life
diminished to quick glances:
what some call progress.

GOOD SHOES

The main difference between those who find
what they seek on the river and those who don't
is simple. But no one tells you how crucial
it is to protect the one thing that carries you

forward with the current, when the water
swirls, stirs up silt to block the eyes
from the history they hunger for, but also
from more recent finds one should avoid.

Thus, with frustrating regularity,
many adventurous mud-slicked sticks
reach up from their beds in the cloudy drink
to persuade the sole of a thin rubber boot

or innocent bare foot that they belong
in here, honestly, it's true—
You have been warned.
This could happen to you.

ASSUMPTIONS FOR SAFETY

In every odd current
look for snakes on the surface

Your boots are not tall enough
yet

Thunder means get to ground

Keep walking

Be ready to swim

WHAT THE RIVER KNOWS

Here we are
my hand is a wing
your skin the sky.

-Harley Elliott, *First Contact*

Water is the memory vault of the world.
When we find tracks at shore's edge
or a small flint hide scraper
meant for just a few fingers

what we really see
is a blink, captured, time
opening its eyes for a moment
and storing the vision away.

We are but feathers brushing
skin that knows the memory—
yes, even ours—
of the world's every touch.

TYLER ROBERT SHELDON is the author of five other poetry collections including *Driving Together* (Meadowlark Books, 2018). He is Editor-in-Chief of *MockingHeart Review*, and his work has appeared in *The Los Angeles Review, Pleiades, Thorny Locust, Tinderbox Poetry Journal, The Dead Mule School of Southern Literature,* and other places. A Pushcart Prize nominee and winner of the Charles E. Walton Essay Award, Sheldon earned his MFA at McNeese State University. He lives in Baton Rouge with his spouse, the artist and upholsterer Alex Arceneaux.

ALSO BY TYLER ROBERT SHELDON

Consolation Prize (Finishing Line Press, 2018)
Driving Together (Meadowlark Books, 2018)
Traumas (Yellow Flag Press, 2017)
First Breaths of Arrival (Oil Hill Press, 2016)

WITH JAMES BENGER

Against the Dark: Road Poems
(Stubborn Mule Press, 2019)

CPSIA information can be obtained
at www.ICGtesting.com
Printed in the USA
BVHW031741240521
607998BV00007B/1203